Lt. Bernadette
and Paramedic Walter's
School Adventure

Authored/Illustrated
by Walter Dusseldorp

D1518994

Honoring Lt. Bernadette Frae, NYS EMT-Paramedic

As we turn the pages of this book, we want to take a moment to celebrate and express our deepest gratitude to a truly remarkable person—Lt. Bernadette Frae.

For over 30 years, Lt. Bernadette Frae has dedicated her life to serving her community with unwavering commitment and compassion. Her bravery and dedication have touched the hearts of many, and her influence has been felt far and wide.

Through countless celebrations and challenges, we have cheered together, shared tears, and gained life-long experiences. Lt. Bernadette's impact has been profound, not only in saving lives but in making each day brighter for those around her.

She has been an incredible partner and friend, standing by us through thick and thin, embodying the true spirit of service. Her legacy is one of courage, kindness, and an unwavering commitment to making the world a better place.

Thank you, Lt. Bernadette Frae, for your extraordinary service, your friendship, and for inspiring us all with your incredible journey. I am forever grateful for the lives you've touched and the difference you've made now and into the future.

With heartfelt gratitude and admiration,
Walter Dusseldorp, EMT-Paramedic.

About the Author

Walter Dusseldorp, MBA, FACHE, EMT-Paramedic

Walter Dusseldorp is a distinguished professional with an MBA, FACHE designation, and extensive experience as an EMT-Paramedic. He is the founder of The Dutch Mentor where he is dedicated to mentoring and coaching individuals to reach their full potential.

Walter has a deep passion for educating and inspiring the next generation of leaders, aviators, and medics. His commitment to nurturing future professionals is reflected in his engaging mentorship programs, which combine his vast expertise with a genuine enthusiasm for teaching and guiding others.

Through his work, Walter aims to empower aspiring leaders and healthcare professionals to excel in their careers, fostering skills that will serve them well in their journeys. To learn more about Walter's impactful programs and how he can support your professional growth, visit www.thedutchmentor.com.

A Special Visit

It was a bright and sunny morning at Strawtown Elementary School. The students were buzzing with excitement because today was a very special day. Lt. Bernadette, and Walter, caring paramedics, were coming to visit!

"Good morning, class!" Mrs. Adams said with a big smile. "Today, we have two very important guests who are here to teach us something that could save lives!"

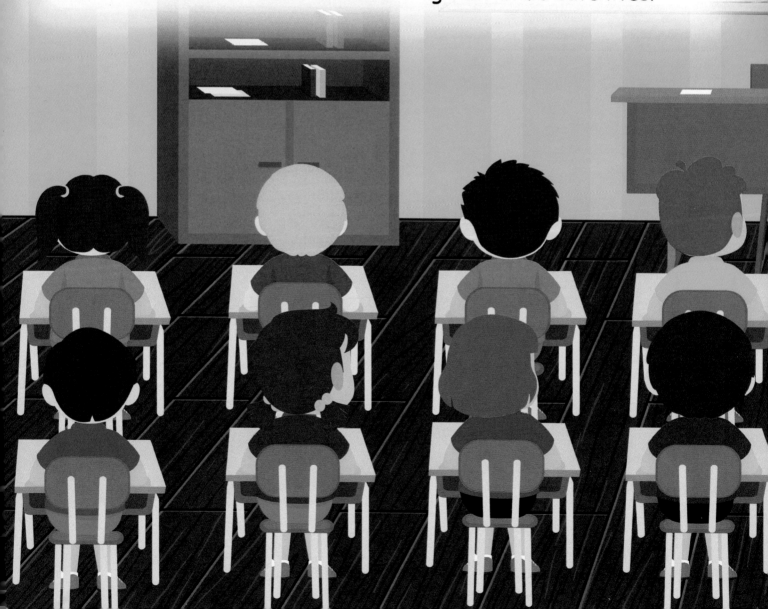

Meeting the Heroes

Lt. Bernadette and Paramedic Walter walked intothe classroom, both wearing their uniforms. The students stared in awe. Lt. Bernadette had a shiny golden badge, and Paramedic Walter carried a medical bag full of interesting tools.

"Hi, everyone!" Lt. Bernadette greeted. "I'm Lt. Bernadette, and this is my friend Paramedic Walter. We're here to talk to you about what to do in an emergency and how to call 911."

"Calling 911 can be scary," Paramedic Walter added, "but we're here to help you understand how important it is and what to expect when you do."

What is an Emergency?

Lt. Bernadette began by asking, "Does anyone know what an emergency is?"

A few hands shot up, and a little girl named Maia answered, "It's when something bad happens, and you need help fast!"

"That's right, Maia!" Lt. Bernadette said. "An emergency is when someone is hurt, very sick, or there's danger like a fire.' When you see something like that, it's time to call 911."

How to Call 911

"Do any of you know how to dial 911?" Paramedic Walter asked.

The students nodded eagerly.

"Great! Now, let's practice together," he said."Imagine you're at home, and you see someone sleeping in the kitchen and you can't wake them up. What would you do?"

A boy named Max raised his hand and said, "I would get my mom, and we'd go outside!"

"Excellent!" Lt. Bernadette replied. "And once you're safe outside, you would use the phone to dial 911. When the operator answers, you need to stay calm and tell them your name, what the emergency is, and where you are."

What to Say to the 911 Operator

"Now let's pretend I'm the 911 operator," Paramedic Walter said with a friendly smile. "You just called because there's a fire in your house. What would you say?"

A shy boy named Jack raised his hand. "Um, I'd say, 'There's an emergency at my house! My name is Jack, and I'm at 123 Maple Street.'"

"That's perfect, Jack!" Paramedic Walter said. "It's very important to know your address so we can find you quickly."

When the Paramedics Arrive

Lt. Bernadette continued, "Once you've called 911,
help is on the way. But what happens
when the paramedics arrive? What should you do?"

A girl named Kate asked, "Should we let them in
and show them where the hurt person is?"

"Yes, exactly!" Paramedic Walter said.
"When we arrive, we'll ask questions to understand
what happened. It's important to listen to us and
answer our questions so we can help the person who's hurt or sick."

How to Stay Calm

"Sometimes, emergencies can be a little scary," Lt. Bernadette said softly. "But staying calm helps everyone, including us. If you stay calm, it helps us do our job better."

"What if I'm too scared to talk?" asked a little boy named Scotty.

"That's okay," Paramedic Walter reassured him. "You can take a deep breath and try your best. Remember, we're here to help, and everything will be okay."

A Fun Activity

Lt. Bernadette and Paramedic Walter decided to do a fun activity with the students. They handed out coloring sheets with a big, friendly phone on them.

"Let's all practice dialing 911 on our pretend phones!" Lt. Bernadette said. "This will help you remember what to do if there's ever an emergency."

The students colored and practiced dialing 911, feeling more confident with every pretend call.

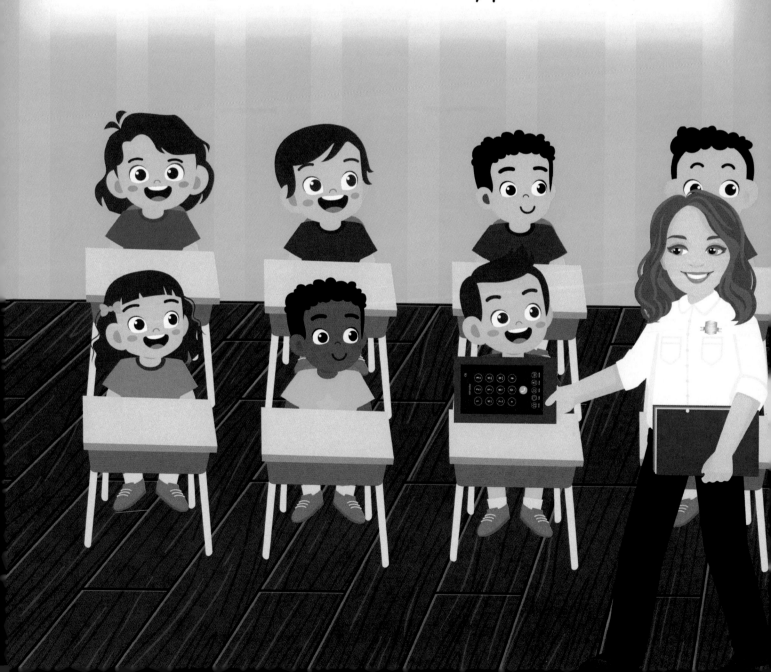

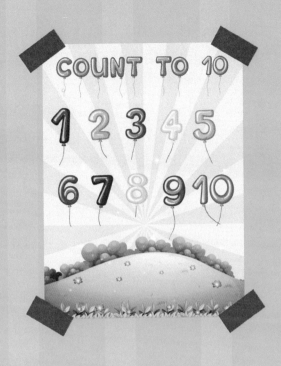

A Special Gift

Before leaving, Lt. Bernadette and Paramedic
Walter handed out special badges to each student.

"These badges are for being brave andlearning how to
help in an emergency," Lt. Bernadette explained.
"Wear them proudly, and remember that you can be a hero too!"

The students beamed with pride as they pinned on
their new badges.

Saying Goodbye

As the visit came to an end, the students clapped and thanked Lt. Bernadette and Paramedic Walter for teaching them such important lessons.

"Remember, you're never alone in an emergency, " Paramedic Walter said with a warm smile. "Help is always just a phone call away."

"And now, you all know how to be brave and smart when it matters most," Lt. Bernadette added. "Thank you for having us, and stay safe!"

With that, Lt. Bernadette and Paramedic Walter waved goodbye, leaving the students feeling empowered and ready to help in any emergency.

Be Prepared!

My name is:

My address is:

My phone number is:

The End

Made in the USA
Middletown, DE
06 December 2024

66249828R00015